Revival

Times of Refreshing

Times of Refreshing

Selwyn Hughes

**CWR, 10 Brooklands Close,
Sunbury-on-Thames,
Middx TW16 7DX**

NATIONAL DISTRIBUTORS
Australia: Christian Marketing Pty Ltd., PO Box 154,
North Geelong, Victoria 3215.
Tel: (052) 786100
Canada: Canadian Christian Distributors Inc.,
PO Box 550, Virgil, Ontario LOS ITO.
Tel: 416 641 0631
Republic of Ireland: Merrion Press Ltd.,
10 D'Olier Street, Dublin.
Tel & Fax: 773316
Malaysia: Salvation Book Centre, (M) Sdn. Bhd.,
23 Jalan SS2/64, 47300 Petaling Jaya, Selangor
New Zealand: CWR (NZ), PO Box 4108,
Mount Maunganui 3030.
Tel: (075) 757412
Singapore: Alby Commercial Enterprises Pte Ltd.,
Garden Hotel, 14 Balmoral Road, Singapore 1025
Southern Africa: CWR (Southern Africa), PO Box 43,
Kenilworth 7745, South Africa.
Tel: (021) 7612560

© CWR 1990
Text originally published 1984, revised and first printed in
this format 1990

Typeset by J&L Composition Ltd, Filey, North Yorkshire

Printed in Great Britain by Richard Clay Ltd,
Bungay, Suffolk

ISBN 1-85345-036-7

All Scripture quotations are from the Holy Bible, New
International Version
Copyright © 1973, 1978, 1984, International Bible Society

CONTENTS

INTRODUCTION   7

Chapter 1:
Revival . . . What is it?   9

Chapter 2:
Revival . . .
The Scriptural Pattern   15

Chapter 3:
Revival . . .
An Extraordinary Happening   19

Chapter 4:
Revival . . .
Seen Through History   29

Chapter 5:
Revival . . .
When does it come?   39

Chapter 6:
Revival . . . How does it begin?   49

Chapter 7:
Revival . . .
What is its purpose?   59

Chapter 8:
    Revival . . .
    The Practical Effects   69

Chapter 9:
    Revival . . . Where it begins   77

Chapter 10:
    Revival . . .
    A Personal Checklist   87

Conclusion:
    Revival . . .
    Preparing The Way   91

Bibliography   94

INTRODUCTION

One of the biggest and most vital issues facing the Church as it pushes open the door into a new decade is this: Are we on the verge of one of the greatest spiritual revivals the world has ever seen? There are evidences that this is so.

In all the years that I have been a Christian I have never witnessed such a burden and expectancy for revival as I do at this moment among the true people of God. Wherever I go I meet prayerful Christians whose spirit witnesses with my own that a mighty Holy Spirit revival is on the way. The 1960's and 1970's were characterised by the word 'renewal'. Then in the eighties, the word began slowly losing currency, and another appeared to take its place – revival. And why? Because great and wonderful though renewal is, many are beginning to see that there are greater things in our Father's storehouse, and slowly but surely their faith is rising to a flashpoint.

Twenty-five years ago, CWR was founded in order to become a voice for revival. Some said at that time that the emphasis was ill-timed as the breath of the risen Christ was already blowing upon the Church in charismatic renewal. Thankful though I was for the showers of renewal that were falling, I still felt that God's call to me was to elevate the spiritual vision of the Church to focus its gaze on revival. At times, and because of the great things that were happening through *renewal*, the message I preached seemed to fall on deaf ears. Now, however, things are different. Almost daily I receive letters from ministers or church leaders that say something like this: "Our church is burdened for revival — how can we prepare ourselves for it?" God, so I believe, is about to send revival to His people — our task is to provide the prayer ramp over which His purposes can pass.

Selwyn Hughes
June 1990

CHAPTER ONE

REVIVAL . . .
What is it?

". . . O Lord, revive thy work in the midst of the years . . ."

(Habakkuk 3:2, AV)

The Holy Spirit is witnessing to many parts of His Church that a spiritual revival is on the way. Probably no greater issue faces the Church at this moment than the issue of revival. Many are very confused about the subject so we must begin by carefully defining the term. We ask ourselves, therefore: What is revival? Before coming to a definite conclusion, it might be helpful if we were to look first at what it is not.

Revival is not evangelism

Great damage has been done by people who insist on placing it in this category. During my first visit to the United States in 1961, I was asked by one group if I would preach at the 'revival' they would be having in their church in a few months' time. I was overwhelmed by what I thought was the faith of the leaders in believing that a revival would take place at a certain time in a certain week until I was informed that, in most American churches, the term 'revival' meant a series of evangelistic meetings, such as I am often invited to preach at in England. But to place revival on a par with evangelism is to misunderstand both its nature and its purpose.

Evangelistic crusades undoubtedly draw thousands to Christ, but, however effective they turn out to be, it will not be revival. Evangelism is the expression of the Church — something brought about by a combination of human and divine effort, but revival is an experience in the Church — something brought about by God alone. Evangelism is the work men do for God: revival is the work God does for men.

Revival is not the restoration of backslidden Christians

There are times in Church life, such as during special conventions, large rallies, conferences, camps and 'deeper-life' meetings, that large numbers of lethargic Christians make a new and deeper commitment to Jesus Christ. This, of course, is highly desirable, and worthy of much praise and gratitude to God — but it is not revival. In one meeting at which I was present, about 500 Christians responded to an invitation to make a total commitment to Christ. Later, a report in a Christian newspaper stated: "Revival breaks out at a Deeper Life Conference." It was true that Christians had been individually re-vived, but in the classic sense of the word, it was not strictly a revival.

Revival is not an unusual sense of God's presence resting upon a particular church or fellowship for a number of weeks or months

I have known churches where a great sense of God's presence predominates for a few weeks more than usual, and they come to speak of it as revival. Supernatural things may happen, such as they have never seen before, but in the strictest sense of the word, it cannot be described as revival. While the salvation of sinners, the restoration of backsliders, and an unusual sense of God's presence hovering over a congregation for a period of time are by-products of revival, these experiences by themselves do not necessarily constitute it. You can see people converted, renewed, restored, and yet fall short of revival. Revival includes all these things, yet it surpasses them all.

Revival is . . .

It is important to remember that any definition can never adequately describe the true nature of revival. "Revival in a definition," said one preacher, "is like David in Saul's armour — it just doesn't fit." Revival, like salvation, is grander and greater and more glorious than anything that can be said or written about it. Having said that, however, we must still struggle to find a working definition of the term. From the Old Testament we see that the word comes from the root meaning 'to live'. The basic idea contained in the word is the return of something to its true nature and purpose. G. Campbell Morgan put it this way: "Revival is the re-animation of the life of the believer (not the unregenerate as they are 'dead in sin') . . . there can only be revival where there is life to revive." A revival, then, is for Christians, not sinners. Sinners don't need revival: they need a resurrection.

Based on these thoughts, I believe the definition of Christmas Evans, the famous Welsh preacher, is the most effective I have ever heard. It is this: "Revival is God bending down to the dying embers of a fire that is just about to go out, and breathing into it, until it bursts again into flame." In revival, men and women come alive to the life of God. D.M. Panton describes it as "the inrush of divine life into a body threatening to become a corpse." The very word *'revival'* suggests that once life existed in all its fullness, but, for some reason, it waned and became moribund. As you no doubt know, when the prefix *'re'* is used in a word, such as *re*vival, *re*animation, *re*turn, and so on, it simply means 'back again'. Revival, then, is the Christian Church going back again to the God-given norm. And what is that 'norm'? Nothing less than the experience of Pentecost.

Peter, in his second sermon, made it clear that when God's people repented of their sin, this would be followed by "times of refreshing from the presence of the Lord" (Acts 3:16). "This phrase," says J. Edwin Orr in his book *The Second Evangelical Awakening in Britain*, "is one of the best definitions of revival in the Bible." Isn't this what happens when true revival takes place? The Church returns to the glory and power that prevailed at Pentecost.

Picture the scene described in Acts 3. Except, of course, for the ministry of Jesus, no prophet had spoken in the nation of Israel for four hundred years. Spiritually the people were at an all-time low — broken, beggared and bankrupt. Then the Spirit came. Thousands were brought into a new and living relationship with God. It was a "time of refreshing from the presence of the Lord". Every revival contains some feature of the Day of Pentecost, for Pentecost is God's pattern of blessing for His Church.

CHAPTER TWO

REVIVAL . . .
The Scriptural Pattern

*". . . Up to that time the Spirit
had not been given, since Jesus
had not yet been glorified."*

(John 7:39, NIV)

In Chapter 1, we said that the pattern for revival is based on the Pentecost experience. Why Pentecost? Why couldn't it be based on an Old Testament revival such as took place under the leadership of Nehemiah, Hezekiah or King David?

The pattern for Old Testament revivals, while powerful and reformative, did not contain enough ingredients upon which to construct a norm. The Holy Spirit — always the prime agent in any revival — worked in a limited capacity in Old Testament times. He came and went, providing temporary infusions of power for temporary tasks. Then again, He came upon people from the outside as opposed to residing permanently on the inside. Further, He could never fully reveal His true nature, for there was no perfect vehicle through whom He could manifest Himself.

John 7:37–44 draws all these strands of thought together into a single statement when he says that the Spirit could not be given until Jesus had been glorified. Why couldn't the Spirit be manifested on earth in all His fullness until Jesus had been glorified? Because only through the life and death of Jesus could God's power be properly seen and understood. Eternal power must be seen not only in the context of signs, wonders and miracles, but at work on a Cross, forgiving its enemies and triumphing over denial, betrayal and an ugly death. It must be seen in supreme modesty and humility — the modesty and humility Jesus showed, when, after triumphing over those who brought about His crucifixion, He chose not to appear in all His glory to make them cower before Him. The power that fell at Pentecost was Christlike power, which became, from that point, the pattern for all future manifestations of power. It is imperative that we grasp this truth, for so many Christians, when praying for revival, set their sights only on the Old Testament pattern. We can certainly learn many valuable lessons and find many challenges from the record of Old Testament revivals, but we must not make them our pattern. The pattern for revival is Pentecost.

The Spirit could not have been fully given in the Old Testament dispensation because this would have set the wrong pattern. The Spirit could not have been fully given in the day of Jesus' humiliation (His birth, life and death), for that, too, would have set the wrong pattern. He could only be given in the day of Christ's triumph — His arrival on the throne — for that alone could set the right pattern.

We must establish this principle in our lives. Our prayers and expectations for revival must be based upon the greatest manifestation of the Holy Spirit the world has ever known — Pentecost. Don't be intimidated by theologians who tell you

---

that Pentecost was simply a one-off experience which God will never want to repeat. The revivals that have taken place in the last few hundred years all contain one or more of the ingredients that were present at Pentecost. In some the dominant feature has been conviction of sin, in others, abounding joy, and in others, amazing supernatural events. Perhaps the next revival will contain *all* the ingredients of Pentecost. Somehow, I think it will.

CHAPTER THREE

REVIVAL . . .
An Extraordinary
Happening

*". . . there came a sound . . . as of
a rushing mighty wind . . . And
there appeared . . . tongues like as
of fire . . ."*

(Acts 2:2–3, AV)

Revival is an extraordinary work of God, producing extraordinary results amongst a large group of people. It is vitally important that we see revival in these terms otherwise we will fall for the popular notion of calling any special activity in the Church by that name.

It has been a long time since the English-speaking world has been visibly shaken by an extraordinary outpouring of the Spirit of God. Most of us have to acknowledge that we have never been part of a deep and powerful revival. That, however, shoud not stop us desiring it, for, with the Acts of the Apostles before us, together with the records of history, we are able to see that God has greater things in store for us than we are presently witnessing and experiencing. Our purpose must be to examine in more detail the ingredients of that first outpouring at Pentecost for there, as we said, we have the model of what God wants His Church to be.

A young Christian said to me some years ago, "I've been a Christian for three months, and as I read the Acts of the Apostles, I sense that something is wrong." "What do you think it is?" I asked. He said, "There seems to be too wide a gap between the Church of that day and the Church of today." He had spotted it. There is! "All revivals," said Dr Martyn Lloyd Jones, "are in some way a return to Pentecost. Every revival in history repeats some aspect of that first great outpouring." The more clearly we understand what happened at Pentecost, the deeper our desire will be for a revival based on God's great pattern — a work of God that is majestic, awesome, startling and extraordinary.

Extraordinary physical occurrences

The first thing that strikes even the most casual reader of the second chapter of Acts is that the descent of the Spirit is accompanied by extraordinary physical occurrences. We read that God sent a "mighty rushing wind" and caused "tongues of fire" to rest on the disciples (Acts 2:2–3). Why, we ask ourselves, did God cause such strange physical occurrences to accompany the descent of the Spirit? The answer is quite clear — God called attention to Himself and His work through unusual physical phenomena.

Some say, of course, that the wind and fire were occurrences that took place only on the Day of Pentecost and were never repeated. That may be so, but similar supernatural happenings took place later in the book of Acts, e.g., Acts 10:44, Acts 19 — events that were most certainly on a par with what happened at Pentecost. The history of revivals, subsequent to the Acts of the Apostles, show that whenever God floods His Church with extraordinary power He usually accompanies it with unusual physical phenomena. Why He should do so is His own business: ours is

---

to make sure that we do not quench the Spirit by our intellectualism and unwillingness to accept the supernaturalism that generally accompanies revival.

Extraordinary preaching

One sermon, preached by Peter, resulted in three thousand souls coming into the kingdom of God (Acts 2:41). Richard Owen Roberts, in his book on revival, says that there are three kinds of preaching. (1) Mouth to ear preaching. This takes place when the words from the mouth of the preacher enter the ears of the hearer but go no further. (2) Head to head preaching. This is where the thoughts of the preacher influence the thoughts of the hearer, affecting the mind, but nothing more. (3) Heart to heart preaching. This is where something happens in the preacher's heart of so compelling a nature that it runs like quicksilver into the heart of the hearer, producing great and wonderful results. That was the kind of preaching that took place at Pentecost.

In revival, preachers experience an extraordinary dynamic flowing through their words. Simple statements and sentences bristle with a strange and unusual power. Men and women are cut to the quick with conviction. You may have heard preaching that has come very close to this, but, believe me, it is nothing compared to what one hears in revival.

An extraordinary sense of God's holiness

Something of this is undoubtedly present in the Church at all times, but when revival comes, the sense of God's holiness is greatly heightened. Such was the sense of God's holiness in the early Church that on one occasion we read: "No-one else dared join them, even though they were highly regarded by the people" (Acts 5:13, NIV).

Every great move of God since Pentecost has contained this impressive ingredient. It is probably true to say that the very first evidence that revival is present is when men and women are gripped by a heightened sense of God's awesomeness and holiness. Conduct, that hitherto appeared respectable, now seems unbelievably wicked. Prejudices that characterised professing Christians for years are seen as grievous sins. Private indulgences, upon which people have looked with favour, suddenly seem to merit all the wrath of God. Prayerlessness, ignorance of Scripture, sins of omission, pride, self-centred living, long-forgotten sins against members of the Body of Christ, words carelessly spoken are no longer defended by a myriad of excuses, but are laid open before the God 'with whom we have to do'. People who thought themselves worthy of heaven stand amazed that they are not in hell.

An extraordinary understanding of the Cross

I doubt whether Peter really understood the meaning of the Cross until it was revealed to him by the Spirit on the Day of Pentecost. Doubtless its meaning deepened for him as he waited with the others those ten days in the Upper Room, but the full understanding of it came only as the Holy Spirit revealed it to him on that first Day of Pentecost. Empowered by the Spirit, he was able to make its meaning clear to the crowd gathered before him, some of whom, no doubt, had actually been present at the Saviour's crucifixion. After Peter's sermon, such was their understanding of the Cross, they were "cut to the heart and said . . . 'Brothers, what shall we do?'" (Acts 2:37, NIV).

The Cross of Christ always takes on a new and precious meaning in times of revival. Awakened hearts see the Cross, not in general terms, but in personal terms. It is no longer "He died for the sins of the world", but "He died for *me*". The Cross becomes so personal that the wounds, bruises and stripes Jesus received, along with the insults, the taunts and the jeers, provoke deep personal sorrow that He had to endure such agony for "such a one as me". These stirrings in the hearts of revived Christians drive the soul to contemplate the Cross in a way never before known. All the devils in hell and all the wickedness on earth do not have the power to keep the awakened Christian from deeper consecration and devoted love to such a Saviour.

An extraordinary interest in prayer and in the reading of the Scriptures

Prior to Pentecost the disciples — Jews to a man — no doubt spent a good deal of their time praying and pondering the Scriptures. After Pentecost, however, both prayer and the study of God's Word took on a new and greater meaning. So important did this become that they decided to abstain from their administrative tasks in order to give themselves continually to prayer and the ministry of the Word. If it be said that these men were the ministers of the Early Church, and as such were obligated to spend their time in this way, then consider the Christians of Berea of whom it was said that they "searched the scriptures daily, whether those things were so" (Acts 17:11).

In today's Church, many Christians are content to let their pastors or elders do the praying and studying for them, but in revival each Christian finds their heart leaping toward prayer and the perusal of the Word of God. They learn to appreciate not only the "sincere milk of the word" but the "strong meat" also, and delight in lengthy, reverent, searching study of God's Word, and in the application of its truths to their lives. Prayer, too, which prior to revival might have seemed a drudgery becomes pure delight. Those words of the hymn, "the sweet hour of prayer", become a precious reality. And when the allotted time for prayer is up, instead of relief that the chore is over, there is sorrow that

---

the time has passed so swiftly. In revival, men and women enjoy, as Moffatt puts it in 1 Samuel 21:7 — being "detained in the presence of the Eternal."

An extraordinary fervour and excitement

One has only to read the pages of the Acts of the Apostles to feel the throb of excitement and joy that characterised the early disciples. It surfaces in many places, one of which is in Acts 8:1-8.

The Early Church was excited about every-thing that was connected with God and His Kingdom. They were excited about Jesus, about the coming of the Spirit, about the establishing of His kingdom, and about His coming again. The dull apathetic attitude, which is present in so many churches today, was a thing unknown in the first century Christian community. They were gripped by intense earnestness and a spirit of expectation. The God that raised up Jesus from the dead had raised them also from their own graves of sin. The power that had elevated Christ to the heavens and placed Him at the right hand of the Father was working in them with all its quickening might.

In revival, Christians often have to defend themselves against the charge that they are drunk (Acts 2:13–14). And what are the marks of a man who is a little drunk? He is happy, hearty, jocular, exhilarated, genial and exuberant. Most of today's Christians do not come under the same dark suspicion as did our first century brothers and sisters, but it is hardly to our credit to stress such a distinction. We are more dignified, more sophisticated, more respectable and more sober — and more in need of revival.

CHAPTER FOUR

REVIVAL . . .
Seen through
History

*". . . I will pour out my Spirit on
all people . . ."*

(Joel 2:28, NIV)

Having examined the ingredients of an extra-ordinary movement of God's Holy Spirit, we turn now to ask ourselves the question: Can we expect these same ingredients to be seen in the Church subsequent to Pentecost? I believe we can. In fact, God has been pleased to show us, in almost every century of the Church, that what He did at Pentecost, He can do again.

I want to examine with you some of the great revivals of history with a view to identifying in them the same characteristics that were present on the Day of Pentecost and in the life of the Early Church. Some might feel hesitant about looking outside the Bible for confirmation of what we are saying, but I believe there is a clear Biblical principle we can follow. God, knowing how easy it is for the human mind to forget even as great and significant an event as the crossing of the Jordan, commanded Joshua to raise up a mem-orial of twelve stones, so that when future generations asked what they meant, they could be told precisely what happened (Joshua 3:9 — 4:7). How sad it is that the great events of the past — even spiritual events — can be so easily forgotten. God has done great things for us in the past and if we ignore them, we do so to our peril. I propose to raise up before you some 'memorial stones' from some of the great revivals of history, in the hope that as you gaze at what God has done, you will draw fresh inspiration from it and move forward with renewed faith and greater expectancy.

Looking back can sometimes be a wasteful exercise, but not when we focus upon the great spiritual events of history. Dr Martyn Lloyd Jones once said, "So dulled is the human mind by sin that we would forget the death of Christ were it not for the fact that God has commanded us to remind ourselves of it regularly by breaking bread and drinking wine." We shall look together at some of the revivals of the past in order to see how every revival is, to some extent at least, a return to Pentecost.

In the previous chapter, we saw that one of the first noticeable features in an extraordinary move of God was *strange and unusual physical manifestations*. This was evidenced in a tremendous way during the 1859 revival in Ulster. The chief characteristic of this revival was, what has come to be called, the 'strikings down'. People would fall to the ground in the streets or in the fields and would lie there motionless for hours. When they recovered, they sensed that God had visited them, and they would worship Him and praise Him with great fervour and excitement. So astonishing was this physical phenomenon that crowds of non-Christians gathered where believers were present just to see these physical manifestations take place. Many were converted as they sensed that God was at work. Our human minds may find it difficult to accept such strange happenings, but we must face the fact that, in revival, God draws attention to Himself by unusual and inexplicable physical manifestations.

Almost every revival carries evidence of very ordinary preachers being transformed as the Spirit came upon them, but perhaps the most conclusive evidence of this is the record of what happened in 1904 to David Davies, a minister in the town of Swansea, South Wales. Prior to the revival, David Davies was known to be a fine Christian minister, but he was regarded by most as an extremely poor speaker. He would cough and splutter his way through a sermon, and, were it not for the consistent Christian character he bore, many would not have gone to listen to him. Then one day revival hit Swansea, and David Davies became a man transformed. He went into his pulpit the next Sunday, and the people could hardly believe their ears. Gone was the hesitancy and stuttering; instead he spoke with the most amazing authority and power. Following his message that Sunday, hundreds of men and women were converted to Christ and, week by week thereafter, David Davies wielded an exceptional ministry in the power and demonstration of the Spirit. When the revival simmered down the following year, the strange thing was that David Davies reverted to his previous hesitant style of preaching. This underlined, even more clearly, the fact that his anointed preaching was not the result of human effort, but a mighty manifestation of the Living God.

It would be impossible to find any revival in history where *an extraordinary sense of God's majesty and holiness* was not present. Just as God's awesomeness and holiness were made known to the Early Church, so they have been made known in every great spiritual awakening since.

One example of this is found in the great revival under Charles Finney in America during the mid-18th century. As Finney preached on such subjects as "The holiness of God" or "Sinners in the hands of an angry God", men and women were given such a revelation of God's holiness that the thought of remaining in a state of sinfulness became intolerable, and they would cry out: "O God, save me from myself and from my sin. Slay me, but do not let me persist another day in this awful condition." Some have put this down to Finney's eloquence and logic, but eloquence and logic, apart from the anointing of the Spirit, are utterly powerless to bring about lasting change in a human heart.

In one service in Northampton, Massachusetts, such was the anointing on Finney's message that the whole congregation of about five hundred people rose up as one man crying out: "O God, we are not worthy to stand in Your presence. Save us — or destroy us." Such was the revelation of God's holiness during the days of Finney that anyone who committed sin would make an instant confession of it. Christians, particularly, feared to enter a church with unconfessed sin in their hearts, unless, in front of the congregation, their sin might be made known.

In the previous chapter, we identified *a new insight into the Cross* as an ingredient of the first Pentecostal outpouring, and it has been present in every revival since.

One such revival in which the work of Christ on the Cross was most significantly underlined was that which took place under the ministry of Christmas Evans in North Wales during the mid-eighteenth century. Christmas Evans had always been an eloquent and forceful speaker, but when the revival came, it touched his tongue with an even greater eloquence and power. The main emphasis in all his preaching was the work of Christ on the Cross. One of his favourite texts was John 3:16, "For God so loved the world, that he gave his only begotten Son ..." When he came to the part of his message that dealt with Christ's death on the Cross, his rugged features would take on a softness and a gentleness that had to be seen to be believed, and his voice, usually stern and demanding, became soft, mellow and persuasive.

A biographer says of him: "Thousands who heard Christmas Evans, having been content to wear the Cross as an ornament, now found themselves viewing it as the place on which Christ bore their own personal sins. The conviction was borne home to every man and woman, that their very own sins put Christ there. In every place he preached, multitudes would weep at the foot of the Cross, and end up wholly saved and redeemed." Can there be any movement of the Holy Spirit in which the Cross is not made prominent? Such a thing is unthinkable. It is as impossible as a river without a source, or a day without light.

Another common element in any revival is that of *an intense interest in prayer and the reading of the Scriptures*. This manifested itself at Pentecost, and it was demonstrated in the more recent revivals of history. A classic example is the revival which happened in Wales at the beginning of this century. When the fire fell, as the Welsh like to put it, one of the first indications that God was at work was evidenced by people's intense desire to pray and read the Bible. Meetings lasted from ten in the morning until twelve at night. There was little preaching. Singing, testimony, prayer and reading the Bible aloud were the predominant features. Coal miners, thousands of feet below the earth, would gather together during their food breaks, not to eat, but to pray and read the Scriptures aloud. Some would even gather at the pithead an hour before work in order to sing and pray. Often the manager and officials of the mine would join in.

This is characteristic not only of the Welsh revival, but of every revival. When God comes down upon His people in the way we are describing, it invariably happens that, instead of excuses for not praying and reading the Scriptures, revived Christians find no other activity so delightful and beneficial. Why should this be so? Simply because the revived Christian has fallen in love. The prime desire of every lover is to be with his beloved. He delights to talk to her, to spend time with her, to listen to her voice, to focus on her endless charm. And so it is with revival.

We consider now the last of these character-istics — *extraordinary fervour and excitement*. We have already spoken of the 1859 revival which, measured by its impact on both the Church and the world, was one of the greatest outpourings of God's Spirit since the Day of Pentecost. The 1859 revival is sometimes called the 'International Revival' because it broke out simultaneously in America, Ulster and many other places. Once people had repented of their sins, and had found perfect peace with God, it invariably happened that they would be filled to overflowing with deep and lasting joy.

Let no one think that revival is associated with gloom and heaviness and a downcast spirit. There is always a period of mourning for sin, but this is soon followed by waves of endless delight and joy. It is surely amongst the most tragic misrepresentations of truth when historians write that, in times of revival, Christians act like "dejected melancholiacs". It is a travesty of the true tradition of revival. Revival imparts an immense sense of well-being. It produces a witness in the hearts of believers that all is well within. It makes music inside the soul, and bestows a glad exuberance. Compare what I am saying with the dull, apathetic attitude which is common in many parts of today's Church. Only the Almighty can produce the change.

O God, send a revival.

CHAPTER FIVE

REVIVAL . . .
When does it come?

"*. . . for it is time to seek the Lord, until he comes . . .*"

(Hosea 10:12, NIV)

We must consider another important question in relation to the subject of revival, when does revival usually come? The answer is simple — when the Church is in declension, or at a low ebb spiritually. It is my belief that we are at such a place right now.

"But surely that cannot be," says someone. "After more than two decades of charismatic Christianity, when thousands of Christians have been renewed, the Church at last has turned a corner. She is on the way to spiritual greatness and supremacy." Not so. Despite the renewal that has taken place and the great activity in the realm of evangelism — things for which we are indeed thankful — the reality is that, generally speaking, the Church in the West is on the decline. Every year denominations report great reduction in numbers, and the Church's influence in the world grows less and less.

The patient may have all the outward signs of good health, but when proper tests are given, the results show cause for deep concern. Don't be misled, I beg you, by the sabre rattling that goes on in today's Church. We sing, we shout, we hold occasional large meetings and conferences, but when it is all over, what impact have we made on society? Some perhaps, but far less than we ought. "Success," said someone, "is measured not by what we are, but by what we are, compared to what we could be.'' All the good we accomplish is nothing compared to what needs to be accomplished. The world laughs at our attempts to influence it. It sees us as weak, feeble and ineffectual.

As far as the Church in the West is concerned, there are signs that it is fast declining and losing its influence in the world. Why? We need to explore and face the issues concerned.

Prayer

The Church of today, generally speaking, is a prayerless Church. Many churches go from week to week without a public prayer meeting of any kind. More upsetting is the fact that many individual Christians have no regular times of private prayer when they commune alone with God. There are exceptions, of course, but in general there is such a perfunctory attitude toward prayer that it is little less than scandalous. The public prayer meeting has often been called 'The Cinderella of the Church', and how fitting that description is of contemporary Christianity. How many churches do you know where as many attend the prayer meeting as the Sunday morning worship service?

"We wish revival would come to us as it came in the Hebrides," said a pastor to Leonard Ravenhill — author of *Why Revival Tarries*. "But revival didn't come to the Hebrides by wishing," said Ravenhill. "The heavens were opened and the mighty power of the Lord shook those islands because a group of people waited, tear-stained and travailing, before the throne of the living God." The birth of a child is preceded by months of burden and days of travail: so is the birth of revival. Jesus prayed for His Church, but then, to bring it to birth, He *gave* Himself in death. It was when Zion *travailed* that she brought forth children (Isaiah 66:8).

Compromise

Another reason why the Church in the West is in a state of decline is because it has compromised its convictions. Why does the Church of the West not suffer for the faith? Dietrich Bonhoeffer said, "Suffering is the badge of the Christian." Luther said, "Suffering is one of the marks of the true Church." Paul said, "All who desire to live a godly life in Christ Jesus will be persecuted" (2 Timothy 3:12, RSV). And Jesus said, "If they persecuted me, they will persecute you" (John 15:20, NIV).

In the light of these statements, I ask again: why does the Church in the West not suffer for the faith? The ugly truth is that we tend to avoid suffering by compromise. Our moral lives are often not much higher than the standards of the world. Our lives do not challenge and rebuke unbelievers by their integrity and purity. The world sees nothing in us to despise. We are seldom bold to rebuke vice or speak out against the injustices in society. Issues like abortion on demand, homosexual practices and other abominations deserve our united condemnation, but many in the Church mind their own business lest people are offended. The Christian message is diluted to such an extent that we escape suffering by compromise.

Suppose we raised our standards, tightened our disciplines, and spoke out against the breaking of God's laws without fear or favour — what would happen? There would be a huge public outcry. We would be ridiculed, scorned and vilified in the press, on radio and on television. But, at the same time, the Church would be carried by God into a place of mighty spiritual revival.

Finance

Yet another evidence for the decline of today's Church is the way in which we rob God of His tithes and offerings. The Church will never be powerful until Christians recognise and understand the principles that govern financial giving. Giving must begin with tithes and offerings to God. No Christian can afford to neglect this. If we give to Him, He has promised that He will "open the windows of heaven" (Malachi 3:10). I am convinced, from the letters I receive, the people I talk to and the reports of others, that multitudes of Christians are robbing God through neglect of tithes and offerings. What is the tithe? The tithe is the first ten percent of our income. This belongs to the Lord. God encourages us to give offerings to meet special needs, but these offerings are above and beyond the tithe. Those who say that tithing is part of the law and does not apply today are quite wrong as the tithe was established before the law was given by Moses (Genesis 14:20), and tithing was reaffirmed by Christ in the New Testament (Matthew 23:23). God also promises that when we are faithful in our tithes and offerings, he "will prevent pests from devouring ... crops, and the vines ..." (Malachi 3:11, NIV).

I am convinced that many of the financial difficulties in which Christians find themselves are due to their failure to tithe. This might sound harsh and legalistic to some, but don't, I beg you, dismiss the principle on those grounds. I have seen it working in my own life and in the lives of many others. Our failure to give tithes and offerings to the Lord will prevent Him from "rebuking the devourer" for our sakes. We will be left to fend for ourselves.

Worldliness

The Church is spiritually declining because of its worldliness. Some think of worldliness as attendance at cinemas, discos, bars, and so on. But worldliness is much deeper than that. You can refrain from attending theatres, cinemas, discos or watching television, and still be worldly. Worldliness is an attitude of mind — it means thinking like the world. And there is evidence that the Church has allowed itself to be squeezed into the mould of the world. Instead of letting Scripture be our standard and guide, we tend to form conclusions based on humanistic thinking — the way of the world. For example, take this issue — one supported not only by the world, but by large numbers of Christians also — that husbands and wives have equal rights and responsibilities in society. Not so, says the Bible. Both are equal before God, but both do not have equal responsibilities: "Wives, submit to your husbands as to the Lord. For the husband is the head of the wife as Christ is the head of the church, his body, of which he is the Saviour. Now as the church submits to Christ, so also wives should submit to their husbands in everything. Husbands, love your wives, just as Christ loved the church and gave himself up for her . . ." (Ephesians 5:22–25, NIV). Take another view held by the world and also by many Christians — the standard for all behaviour is love. No, says the Bible, the standard for behaviour is truth: "Now we know that God's judgment . . . is based on truth" (Romans 2:2, NIV). Take yet another popular view of life, and one supported by many Christians — marriages that are unhappy qualify for divorce. The answer, according to Scripture, is to overcome self-centredness and put one's own interests last: "Do nothing out of selfish ambition or vain conceit, but in humility consider others better than yourselves. Each of you should look not only to your own interests, but also to the interests of others" (Philippians 2:3–4,

NIV). Slowly but surely the Church in this generation is allowing its thinking to be cast in the mould of the world. Apostasy occurs when the world influences the Church. In revival, the Church influences the world.

Unrepentance

What was the urgent note that characterised New Testament Christianity, but is scarcely heard in the Church today? Why, repentance of course! Time after time, in the Acts of the Apostles, the call to repentance was sounded. The preaching of the early apostles was dominated by this theme. The mandatory nature of repentance was woven throughout the entire fabric of the life and ministry of Jesus Himself, and its urgent necessity repeatedly proclaimed. But repentance is a missing note in today's Church. "Nowadays," says James Robinson, an American evangelist, "there is abroad an 'easy believism'. We tell people, 'Say this prayer after me and you will have the gift of eternal life, a mansion on the main street of heaven, a diamond-studded crown, and you will be ruler over five cities in the Millennium.'" An exaggeration? Well maybe, but there is still enough truth in it to hurt.

When men and women are not challenged to repent as they come into the Christian life, then they enter it with their ego still intact and dominant. Is it any wonder that we have so many Christians in the Church today who are argumentative, self-centred and rebellious? They never really surrendered their will when they entered the Christian life, and when any issue comes up between their will and God's will, they, never having learned the way of obedience and repentance, take a self-centred stance — one that is usually in opposition to the Almighty. A church which does not recognise the importance of repentance is a church that is rapidly in decline.

Attitudes

Yet another of these signs is the *unloving attitudes of Christians toward one another*. Some time ago, I wrote to ten Christian leaders in Great Britain, asking if they would share, openly and frankly, where they saw the greatest need for concern in today's Church. All, with one exception, put at the top of his list the harsh, critical and unloving attitudes which Christians have one toward the other. A man I know, who travels the country visiting churches of all denominations, said: "The biggest single issue that muffles the voice of the Church is the hostile and unloving attitudes Christians have one toward another." The truth is that such unloving attitudes can never be entirely eliminated from the Church by powerful preaching, expert counselling, or by writing about it. These things can help, but the real answer lies in a mighty Holy Spirit revival that cleanses the Church of all its blemishes and impurities, and gives it once again a powerful voice in the world.

We must conclude our examination of the

signs and evidences of today's declining Church. Although, as we have been saying, there is a great deal of zeal and activity in today's Church, it has, nevertheless, the smell of decay upon it. This is evidenced in its general attitude of prayerlessness, its tendency to imbibe the attitudes of the world, its willingness to compromise, its disregard of God's principles of finance, its failure to preach and practise the truth of wholehearted repentance, and the unloving attitudes of Christians toward one another.

Our condition is desperate, but, take heart, for, as Peter Lewis says, "Revival comes to a desperate church not a triumphalist one."

CHAPTER SIX

REVIVAL . . . How does it Begin?

". . . Will you not revive us again, that your people may rejoice in you?"

(Psalm 85:6, NIV)

We turn our focus on another important question that has to do with the issue of revival: How do revivals begin? Quite simply, the answer is that revivals begin in the sovereign purposes of God. Man has little to do with them: they are initiated not on earth, but in heaven. There are many things that Christians, by dedicated and spiritual effort, can bring to pass in the Church, but revival is not one of them. We said earlier that evangelism, counselling, preaching, teaching, and other such things are work that men and women do for God. Revival is work that God does for men and women.

It is at this point — the sovereignty of God — that Christians tend to differ in their thinking about revival. One school of thought says: "Revival is a sovereign act of God, and there is absolutely nothing that man has to do with it. God sends revival when He wills and does not consult or confer with any of His creation." Another school of thought says: "Revival can happen any time the Church wants it — providing she is willing to pay the price." Charles Finney believed this. "Revival," he said, "can happen in the Church the moment we are prepared to meet God's conditions."

The truth, as is so often the case, is found, I believe, somewhere between these opposing views. Revival is a sovereign act of God in the sense that He alone can produce it, but it is transported to earth on the wings of fervent, believing prayer. Every revival in history — Pentecost included — began in heaven, but flowed into the Church across the ramp of intercessory prayer. This view, I believe, neither robs God of His sovereignty, nor man of his responsibility. I have thought long and hard on this matter, and I have come to the conclusion that there are two rails running through Scripture — one is the sovereignty of God and the other is the responsibility of man. If you keep to just one of those rails, you end up being derailed. Those who talk only of the sovereignty of God end up minimising the responsibility of man. Those who talk only of the responsibility of man end up minimising the sovereignty of God. When we move along both rails, making sure that we do not place a disproportionate emphasis on either truth, then we are more likely to arrive at sounder judgments and better conclusions.

A single statement by John Wesley, which I have quoted on numerous occasions, has helped me more than anything I have ever read to balance these great truths of the sovereignty of God and the responsibility of man. He said, "God does nothing redemptively in the world — except through prayer."

Can you see what he is saying? Whenever God wants to bring His redemptive purposes to pass here on earth, He does not move arbitrarily but respects the principle of prayer, which He Himself has established. He, therefore, touches the hearts of certain of His people to pray — it may only be a few — and thus proceeds to transmit His purposes along the ramp that prayer has built. God never acts against His nature. He would cease to be God if He did so. And His nature is to use, not ignore, the great principle of prayer which He has so wonderfully established in His universe.

So although, from the divine point of view, revival begins in the sovereign purposes of God, it would be true to say, I believe, that from the human point of view, it begins in the hearts of those who are burdened to see God work in an extraordinary way.

John Wallace, Principal of the Bible College I attended in my youth, used to say: "Before there can be a blessing, somebody has to bear a burden." He went on to illustrate it in this way: "Before deliverance came to the nation of Israel in Egypt, Moses had to bear a burden. Before the great temple of God was built, Solomon had to bear a burden. Before the sins of the world could be removed, Jesus had to bear a burden. *Before there can be a blessing, somebody has to bear a burden.*" This is one of the great principles of Scripture which can be traced right through the Bible from Genesis to Revelation. It can be seen at work, too, in the history of revival.

Before God comes from heaven to work in extraordinary ways, He places the burden of revival on the hearts of certain of His people. Why some should be selected to carry this burden and others not, I cannot say, except that it is a mystery we must ascribe to the sovereignty of God. One thing is sure, however, God never goes over the head of His Church to introduce redemptive changes in His universe. When revival comes to the West, it will come through the hearts of those who have been greatly burdened to pray.

But revival is not only a sovereign work of God: it is a sudden work of God. Revival begins without much preamble and without warning. Pentecost began in this way you remember: "When the day of Pentecost had *come . . . suddenly* a sound came from heaven like the rush of a mighty wind" (Acts 2:1–2, RSV). This is brought out very clearly in the book of Habakkuk (3:1–3). After the prophet has prayed for revival: "O Lord, revive thy work in the midst of the years," the next verse goes on to say: "God came from Teman, the Holy One from Mount Paran." The original Hebrew here, so I am told, conveys the impression of suddenness. Following Habakkuk's prayer, God came suddenly, and without warning, to revive and reinvigorate His people.

When revival came to Ulster in the nineteenth century — it came *suddenly*. When revival came to Wales in 1904 — it came *suddenly*. When revival came to the Hebrides in the middle of this century — it came *suddenly*. Study the record of any revival throughout history and you will find that God came to His people unheralded and unannounced. It sometimes happens that He imparts to a few people a sense of His approaching presence, but the actual breakthrough always comes with startling suddenness. Tonight we may go to sleep aware that the Church desperately needs revival, and wake up tomorrow to find ourselves right in the middle of it. Oh, that it may be so.

Revival also begins in the most unlikely places. Pentecost, you remember, began not in the majestic atmosphere of Solomon's Temple, but in an Upper Room. For some reason, God seems to delight in bypassing the places where we might expect revival to break out — in a splendid cathedral or at a large Christian conference — and causes His fire to burst out in a small prayer meeting where only a few are present. In fact, no revival has been an official movement of the Church. This is why revival always astonishes the Church — it flares up where it is least expected.

Have you ever heard of the Primitive Methodist revival in the 1800's? This began not on the historic sites of former Methodist accomplishments, such as in London or Bristol, but in a tiny hamlet on the hillside of Mow Cop near Stoke-on-Trent. Someone described it as the "least likely place in which a revival has ever broken out". And why? Because there were only a few grey, roughly built cottages situated there, inhabited by people with little intellectual ability or learning. The area was bleak, rugged and uninteresting. Nevertheless, this is the place God chose in which to manifest His power and glory. If ever the Church receives a blow to its pride, it is when God breaks forth in revival. He shows, in that act, how unimpressed He is with ornate buildings or exquisite architecture. When God came down to meet Moses in Midian, did He do so because Midian was a holy and sanctified place? No, He came not because it was holy, but to *make* it holy (Exodus 3:1–5).

One revival in North Wales in the eighteenth century began in the most unexpected way with the death of a highly-respected minister. As the crowds gathered at his funeral service, the Holy Spirit broke in and produced a mighty revival. The 1904 revival is connected with the name of Evan Roberts, but it really began in a meeting at which Evan Roberts was present, when a shy and timid 16 year-old girl stood up and blurted out, "I love Jesus Christ with all my heart."

Consider again the great revival which took place in New York in 1847. A Dutch business-man, Jeremiah Lanphier, advertised a midday prayer meeting in his office. At the first meeting, six people were present. So mightily did the Spirit work amongst those six, that within six months more than 100,000 businessmen were crowding into prayer meetings all over the city. In Uganda, a revival broke out when one Christian walked more than a hundred miles to ask the forgiveness of a Christian whom he had wronged twenty years previously.

The question is often asked by those who study the origin of revival: Why does God bypass organisations, committees and the well-oiled machinery of the Church in order to bring a revival to birth? He does it so that the glory might not be man's, but God's. The Almighty delights to be involved in situations where there is no doubt who is responsible for the victory which has been achieved. And revival is such a situation.

Revivals begin not only in the most unlikely places and in the most unexpected ways, but also with the most unassuming people. Don't think, when you read of famous names such as Charles Finney, Christmas Evans, and so on, that all revivals begin with such outstanding person-alities. In fact, although revivals have marked the history of the Church throughout its long course of almost twenty centuries, most of these began with unknown individuals. And those who were well-known, generally speaking, played little part in the revival until they themselves had passed through a time of deep repentance and inner cleansing.

Ever heard of James McQuilkee? I'll be surprised if you have. Yet he was a man whom God used mightily in the Ulster revival in 1859. Have you heard of David Morgan? God used him greatly in one of the revivals that shook Wales, yet prior to the revival he was known to no more than the five hundred or so people who lived in the small village where he was brought up. In researching this subject, I came up with names of men who never merited a mention in the usual books on revival, but who were used by God nevertheless to bring about His mighty purposes here on earth.

I am conscious, as I write, that within me is a tendency to try to explain why God works in this strange way, but the Spirit seems to be saying to my heart: "Don't try to explain my ways, for they are higher than your ways, and my thoughts higher than your thoughts. If you can explain a revival — then it is not a revival."

CHAPTER SEVEN

REVIVAL . . . What is its Purpose?

"Praise be to his glorious name forever; may the whole earth be filled with his glory . . ."

(Psalm 72:19, NIV)

What is the purpose of revival? Why does God send these periodic awakenings? Those who have made a special study of revival tell us that in every century of the Church, somewhere or other in the world, a revival containing one or more of the features of the first Pentecost has taken place. Again we ask: What is God's purpose behind these great awakenings? The primary purpose behind every spiritual revival is to bring glory to God's Name. Lose sight of this and you can miss your way regarding this great and important subject.

Many Christians are motivated to pray for revival because they are tired of the dull, apathetic condition of the Church, and long for the kind of meetings revival produces — meetings in which there is great spiritual fervour and excitement. There is no doubt that revival creates such an atmosphere, but if that is our primary motivation, then we have simply fallen prey to the age-old problem — self-centred interests.

But someone asks: Isn't it legitimate for Christians to enjoy themselves in God's presence, and to long for services which pulsate with divine power? Yes, of course it is — this is certainly a legitimate desire. The problem arises when that desire takes priority, for then your interests, and not God's, take pre-eminence. I say again, the primary purpose behind every spiritual revival is to bring glory to God's Name. When we make His goal our goal, then we bring ourselves in line with His infinite purposes. And when we are linked to His purposes, we are linked to His power. The main purpose of our being in the world, and in the Church, is not to enjoy ourselves, but to glorify God. God's glory is to be the goal — enjoyment the result. Reverse the order and you end up in conflict with God, and with the structure of the universe.

Some of the great theologians of the past, when laying down guidelines for the worship of the Church, asked the question: "What is the chief end of man?" With absolute accuracy and splendid conciseness, they answered: "Man's chief end is to glorify God, and to enjoy Him forever." Any pursuit of pleasure, even spiritual pleasure, apart from God who made us, is a violation of God's purpose in the creation of man, and a travesty of man's best interests. Man was not made for himself but for God.

"To pursue self-gratification to the abandonment of God," the theologians went on to say, "is to guarantee immediate disappointment and eventually total ruin." Now don't dismiss this as mere theological rhapsodising: it is an important point. The greatest need of the Church at this moment is to put God's interests first, and other interests second. Some may be prepared to pray earnestly for revival, fearing that if it doesn't come, their very way of life will be undermined or destroyed. Others may pray for revival motivated by a concern for loved ones who are in sin. Still others may pray for revival out of a concern for the bankrupt condition of the Church. But worthy as such aims may be, let it be understood that the primary reason why we should pray for and desire a spiritual revival is for the glory of God.

A second purpose for which God sends revival is to elevate His Church to the level of power it was always intended to enjoy. The history of the Church has been one of 'peaks and troughs'. At times it soars in the chariot of revival with the world at its feet. Other times it is beggared and bankrupt — the laughing stock of society. History records that 50 years after Pentecost, the Church began to lapse into lukewarmness and infidelity, and by the end of the first century had lost much of its spiritual supremacy. It stayed this way for over a century. Then at the beginning of the third century, God stepped in to revive His people. In subsequent centuries, this pattern of 'peaks and troughs' is clearly traceable. During one period the Church is up, in the next, it is down. Then when it looks as if it is finished and will never rise again, God graciously steps in and touches the hearts of His people in revival power.

Why should it be that with all the great ministries which God sets in the Church — gifted pastors, teachers, prophets, and so on — it should fall into periods of lukewarmness and declension?

There can only be one answer — the wayward-
ness of the human heart. Such is the human
condition that even the most spiritual people can
allow their hearts to be turned away from God by
things such as materialism and humanism. So
wilful are their desires that the ordinary ministries of the Church cannot move them. It is at
such times that God sends revival.

As we continue meditating on one of the
reasons why God sends revival, to elevate His
Church to the position it was always intended to
enjoy, a question is raised which we will look at
in greater detail later: Is the Church at present
experiencing all that God intends for her?
Hardly. Someone has described the Church here
in Great Britain as 'a sleeping giant'. "But how
can that be," asks someone, "when the Church in
general is caught up in a tremendous amount of
evangelistic activity for the last decade of the
century. Isn't this evidence that the 'sleeping
giant' has awakened?" Not necessarily. Any
evangelistic concern is good and proper and has
my support one hundred percent. When I use the
term 'sleeping giant', I am using it in relation to
what the Church could be doing, not in relation
to what it is doing. When revival comes, the
'sleeping giant' will not just stir and awaken, but
will move with such dynamic power and impact
that it will make a mass evangelistic crusade look
like a Sunday School picnic.

Imagine your church with every member
living together in harmony, with not one

sleeping Christian left, with every individual on fire for God, and with everyone intent on seeing the will of Christ accomplished. To this startling picture, add the power that produced such astonishing scenes on the Day of Pentecost. Now multiply this until it fills every church in every community, every town, every city in the nation. Unleash all this mighty power against the forces of sin and evil, THAT is revival!

God sends revival in order to arrest the attention of an unbelieving world. We have to face the fact that, at the moment, the world hardly recognises the presence of the Church. It pays lip service to it, of course, but deep down unbelievers regard the Church as a relic of the past — archaic and ineffectual. This finds expression in many ways. When a minister is portrayed in a play, he is invariably a stilted caricature of the real thing, a dyspeptic creature, who speaks in a silly, affected voice, and who is more non-Christian than Christian. It would be impossible to deny, of course, that occasionally one meets members of the clergy who come close to the caricature, but to reason from the particular to the general is foolish and absurd.

Another idea the world has of the Church is that we are a group of psychologically immature people needing a religious prop in order to face the challenge of living in a strife-torn world. But that isn't the worst of it. Men and women in the world project the weaknesses, the mistakes, the inadequacies of the Church on to God, and say:

"If there is a God, what kind of God can He be to give His Name to such a motley crowd as this?" Revival changes all that. It puts God right in the middle of His people, giving them a voice so powerful that when the Church speaks — the world sits up and listens. To those who say that the Church of Jesus Christ is weak and enervated, we can reply: "That is how it may look at present. But just wait — our God is on the way."

Permit me to ask you a personal question: Does it grieve you that we are living in a godless and morally bankrupt age? Does it grieve you that the Name of our God is ridiculed and blasphemed in almost every section of society? Does it grieve you that men scoff at the Bible, this matchless book which God brought into being by the power of His Holy Spirit, and regard it with no more interest than the works of Shakespeare?

The more I see and hear arrogant men denying or blaspheming the very God who gave them breath, the more I can understand and identify with the Psalmist in Psalm 46. The writer penned these words because he was conscious that all around him godless men were repudiating the Almighty by their blasphemous utterances and sinful lives, and he petitions God that such men might be silenced. The Psalmist implores God to do something, to come from heaven and stop the mouths of those who were ridiculing Him. He wants God to rise up and confront an unbelieving world and say: "Be still, and know that I am God" (Psalm 46:10, NIV).

Do not you, too, when you hear the Lord's Name taken in vain, spiritual concerns mocked and eternal issues flippantly treated, feel the way this Psalmist felt? If you are a Christian, and you don't, then, believe me, there is something deeply wrong with you. To hear sacred things treated with contempt and eternal matters trivialised without indignation is not possible to those who truly love God and serve His Son, the Lord Jesus Christ.

One of the purposes of God in sending revival is to make the world sit up and take notice. We turn again to the Day of Pentecost as a classic example of this. We read that when the Holy Spirit fell, the people who were in Jerusalem, together with all the strangers gathered there for the feast, came to where the disciples were, and said, "What does this mean?" They were arrested by the mighty outpouring of God's eternal power. That is always the case in revival — unbelievers, albeit out of curiosity, gather in the presence of the unusual and ask the question: "What does this mean?" (Acts 2:12, NIV).

As a boy I remember hearing a great preacher, who was converted in the 1904 Welsh revival, recounting his experience of conversion. "I was a drunkard and a down-and-out," he said, "but one night someone came into the pub where I was drinking and said, 'There's some strange things going on in the church down the road.

People are crying, falling on the floor, and all kinds of things are happening.' My friends and I went down to the church to scoff and have some fun. But when I entered the door it was as if I had been arrested. I sobered up immediately, and fell to my knees calling upon God to have mercy on my soul." And then he added some words which I have heard on numerous occasions in connection with revival: "I went to scoff but I stayed to pray."

Clearly, there is nothing the Church can do to produce such an impact and an effect. Evangelistic crusades, rallies, concerts can attract and appeal to the world, but only revival can arrest it.

CHAPTER EIGHT

REVIVAL . . .
The Practical
Effects

*"Thy people shall be willing in
the day of thy power . . ."*

(Psalm 110:3, AV)

We turn now to consider another important question in relation to revival: What are its results? We have already touched on some aspects of this, but now we examine the matter in greater depth.

Revival, as we have seen, results in greater power and purity in the Church. But what does this mean in practical terms? First, it means that long-standing habits of self-indulgence, that surrender neither to reason nor to God, will be broken when revival comes. The doors and walls of the prison of self, in which so many Christians are incarcerated, will be broken down by revival. The Lord who came to declare freedom to the captive will enable His people to be free indeed. Unconfessed sins that have been covered over for years will be brought to light. The interesting thing about the exposure of sin in times of revival is that the fear and shame which usually accompany such moments are thought of as nothing in comparison with the prospect of forgiveness and cleansing.

Second, it means that the plans and strategies of the Church are thrown into upheaval and disarray. Goals and ambitions once thought to be of the utmost spiritual importance are seen to be but temporal. God's timing, God's purpose, God's plans rule the day. Some church structures may collapse when revival comes, but are then rebuilt "according to the pattern shown in the Mount" (Hebrews 8:5, AV). Traditions may perish. Programmes may have to be abandoned and schedules rearranged. Well-rehearsed choir numbers may remain unsung for ever. Nothing is ever the same again in the Church when revival comes.

A third result of revival is the breaking of the will. When God moves from heaven in extraordinary power, all that stands in opposition to Him may be expected to be broken and cast aside. Pastors, elders and leaders will be broken by revival. Men who have preached interesting and eloquent sermons may discover their ministry has the value of "wood, hay and stubble". Sermons and messages which seemed satisfactory enough in previous days will never do for revival. God, the Master Workman, will break the congregation, too. Men and women, who had resisted Him and His Word, now find themselves pliant and ready to do His bidding. But the breaking always leads to a remaking. God not only pulls down — He builds up.

A fourth result of revival among the people of God is that holiness becomes the prime object of their lives. To be like Jesus often becomes the theme song of a revival. Christians are consumed with a desire to conform to Christ's image, and the principle of Romans 8:29 — "God decided that those who came to him . . . should become like his Son" (TLB) — becomes the dominating passion of their lives. The great truths of Scripture are no longer relegated to group discussions in church on a Sunday or in a mid-week house group, but are lived out on a daily basis and applied in every exigency of life. Revived people are truly a holy people.

A fifth result of revival is that Christians become greatly burdened for the souls of unbelievers. Prayer for the eternal welfare of those outside of Christ becomes a passion. Someone said that the word that is characteristic of revival is the word 'Oh'. It comes out continually in the prayers of those who agonize for the lost. "*Oh* God," they cry, "save those who are dying in sin." Nothing short of lasting conversions will satisfy the saints in a time of revival. They pray that the same liberating Spirit that broke and remade them will do the same in the hearts of their friends, families, acquaintances and people throughout the world. New converts are made without arm–twisting. No elaborate plans for follow-up are necessary as new converts stand on their own feet from the moment of conversion.

A sixth result of revival is that Christians begin to manifest the love of Christ toward one another. Those who have borne grudges or have gossiped about other Christians go to those they have wronged and ask for their forgiveness. Maintaining a clear conscience becomes a matter of paramount importance. Those who have sinned privately make their confession to God whom they have wronged. Those who have sinned publicly find the grace and strength to make a public confession. A watching world will look on in amazement as it sees Christians, who had hitherto lived hypocritical lives, now take their faith seriously. The light that shines in a revived Church cannot be put out. It shines more and more until the perfect day.

As we continue meditating on what we can expect to happen when revival comes, we turn our attention away from its effect upon the Church, and consider how it affects the wider community and ultimately the nation.

Some people say that revival is completely irrelevant to such issues as politics and socio-economics, but to hold such a view is to fly in the face of the facts. J. Edwin Orr in his book, *The Second Evangelical Awakening in Britain*, says that when revival came to Wales "drunkenness was immediately cut in half and many public houses went bankrupt. Crime was so diminished that the judges were presented with white gloves signifying that there were no cases of murder, assault, rape, robbery, or such like, to consider. The police became 'unemployed' in many districts. Stoppages occurred in coal mines, not due to unpleasantness between management and workers, but because so many miners became converted and stopped using foul language that the horses which hauled the coal trucks in the mines could no longer understand what was being said to them, and transportation ground to a halt."

In an age when so much is being said about the Church's duty to become involved in bringing about positive social and political changes, it is salutary to observe the tremendous effects which God's people have had upon society when they are in a state of revival. When the Church communicates her unique message in the power of the Holy Spirit, an improved society is always an early and inevitable result. Those who are not even converted sense a heightening of morality, and are strangely restrained and affected by it.

At this moment, thousands of Christians throughout the world are deeply concerned over the high rate of abortion. Despite our strongest protests, we seem powerless to get people to see that life begins at the moment of conception, and that to abort a foetus for any other reason than danger to the life of the mother is an offence in the eyes of God. Though the problem is one that did not affect previous generations to such a degree, and we have no statistics against which we can measure it, I believe, nevertheless, that revival in the Church would greatly affect the thinking of society in relation to this issue. The Holy Spirit flowing out from the Church into the world with power would, in my judgment, cause men and women to feel deeply uncomfortable about abortion. In no time, the laws governing abortion on demand would be changed.

Today subjectivism has taken the place of fixed principles of moral law. Instead of judging conduct on the basis of what God says, we now say: "Let your conscience be your guide." But conscience, without the reinforcement of God's Word and the Holy Spirit, can excuse just as easily as it can accuse. Revival would not force men and women to act in ways that are consistent with God's demands in Scripture, but the light it would cast would make men think twice before embarking upon deeds of darkness.

Consider yet another social problem — divorce. Prior to the 1960's, the divorce rate in this country was returned in five-yearly periods. In 1951-56 there were 146,186 divorces — an average of approximately 29,000 a year. Now, because divorce is a matter of immense social concern, the statistics are returned annually. In 1982, the divorce rate in Great Britain and Northern Ireland was 150,000. In two decades, the divorce rate had rocketed! In the following five years it had increased by a further ten per cent to over 165,000 in 1988.

What can be done about this problem? Very little, it seems. The Church can teach about the sanctity of marriage for all it is worth, but this seems to make little difference to a secular society. The community, as a whole, tends to make divorce easier and easier. Revival in the Church would, I believe, curb the rising divorce rate. Such would be the power that would flow through the Church, that its voice would be heeded, and its standards recognised and upheld.

Revival would restore a sense of destiny.

Prior to World War Two, the British people believed they had a special destiny in the world. Some aspects of the idea were, of course, quite insupportable. Those who said that whoever resisted Britain resisted heaven, and old memorial tablets in churches to admirals and generals declare this, were speaking from an imperialistic and not a spiritual perspective. Thankfully, most of that imperial pride has gone. Discerning people know that the only country with a future is the country which sets out to bring its purposes in harmony with the purposes of God.

One Christian historian believes that Britain could do that more swiftly than most other countries. The reasons given are these: "She has a longer history and experience of self-government, and long enjoyment of civil, political and religious liberty has given her a maturity of judgment in all these fields, which is still rare among men. Britain has had no civil war for 300 years. Tolerance, fair play and a freedom from frenzy mark the people. The nation has a high destiny still." A revival in the House of God would inevitably overflow into the Houses of Parliament. Revived Christians in government, and other high places, would speak with new power and new authority. Few, if any, would be able to resist the call to Biblical standards and morality. Yes, our country can be a great nation still — but nothing short of revival in the Church can accomplish it.

CHAPTER NINE

REVIVAL . . .
Where it Begins

*"If my people, who are called by
my name, will humble
themselves and pray . . . and turn
from their wicked ways, then will
I hear . . ."*

(2 Chronicles 7:14, NIV)

Having spent the past eight chapters examining the various aspects of revival, we come now to what is perhaps the most important question of all: What is the way to revival? We said that revival is a sovereign act of God, and that the Church is unable to produce it, unable to explain it, and unable to control it. It is a glorious, majestic, mighty, awesome act of God in which He sweeps His Church from spiritual bankruptcy into spiritual riches.

The impression you may have from reading this book is that as revival is a sovereign act of God, and cannot be produced by anyone on earth, then the only thing the Church can do is sit back and wait for God to send it. Nothing could be further from the truth. Revival is most certainly a sovereign act of God, in the sense that only He can initiate it, but whenever God gets ready to revive His Church, He approaches those who are ready to listen to His voice, and instructs them on how to be the channel through whom His Spirit can flow from heaven to earth.

The instructions God gives to His people, when preparing them for revival, are crystallised in 2 Chronicles 7:14.

This verse has been described as "the final and finished formula on how to prepare for revival". It is so important that I propose to devote a whole chapter to it. Before we begin to look at it clause by clause, let me urge you to spend a few minutes memorising it. If you do, I promise you that this text will make more of an impact upon your life than anything else you have ever experienced.

"If my people, who are called by my name, will humble themselves and pray and seek my face and turn from their wicked ways, then will I hear from heaven and will forgive their sin and will heal their land."

We begin with the opening clause: "*If my people, who are called by my name . . .* " The truth we have been stressing over and over is, once again, brought to our attention, revival begins with the people of God. To criticise and condemn unbelievers for their unbiblical standards and practices is beginning at the wrong place. Revival relates first to the people of God. Some believe that the term 'people of God' refers to all who have some kind of religious inclination. But the Almighty leaves us in no doubt as to whom He is addressing: "If my people, *who are called by my name.*" He is talking to those who know Him intimately, who have taken His Name upon themselves, and who are linked with Him in a family relationship.

What a responsibility it is to belong to the people of God. After all, whether we like it or not, people judge God by the impression we make upon them. If we fail, they don't reason with themselves and say: "He is only one in a million Christians — the others are a good deal better." No, they observe our way of life, evaluate our actions and our behaviour, and say: "If that's what serving God is like, then I want nothing to do with it." This is why God chooses to begin with His own people when He is about to bring His redemptive purposes to pass in history. Once the people of God are right, then it won't take long to put the world right.

"If my people, who are called by my name, will *humble themselves* ..." Humble themselves? Shouldn't prayer take priority of place here? There is good reason why God puts humility first. It is because pride is one of the biggest barriers to God having His way in His Church. Not for nothing did the old theologians put pride at the head of the list of the "seven deadly sins". "Pride," said Dr. W. E. Sangster, "is the primal sin. Little as we know of the life of the angels, there is evidence for believing that pride led to the revolt of Satan in heaven." It certainly is in the vanguard of any revolt we may make against the God of heaven.

Self-centredness is a blight that affects both the redeemed and the unredeemed. Because we are Christians, it does not mean that we are automatically protected from the disease of self-interest. How many times have you, even though you are a Christian, allowed yourself rather than God to have the benefit of the doubt over some spiritual challenge He gave you? When pride is present, then everything which comes up has an immediate self-reference. Me ... Me ... Me ... or I ... I ... I. There can be no real victory in any Christian's life until they have found victory over pride. The phrase, "humble yourselves", suggests that an act of the will is necessary. God can humble us, but how much more meaningful it becomes when we do it ourselves. Are you a proud person? Then do something today to trample on your pride. Pride has many evil characteristics, but its greatest evil is this — it blocks the way to revival.

"If my people, who are called by my name, will humble themselves *and pray* ..." But Christians *do* pray! But how much? How sincerely? How unselfishly? When did we last stay up late just to pray? When did we last get up early simply to pray? Many Christians go through their Christian life praying by rote, or praying only when they want something for themselves. This isn't the kind of praying God means when He lays down the conditions for revival.

One of the greatest definitions of prayer I know is this: prayer is co-operation with God. Consider what is meant by this phrase — co-operation with God. It is an exercise that links our faculties to our Maker to work out the intentions He had in mind in their creation. Prayer isn't bending God's will to ours, but bending our will to His. We work out the purposes which God has worked out for us.

I read the account of a man who sat and listened to an organist playing a beautiful melody. He said that, behind the organ, he could see a man striking upon bells the same notes the organ was playing. So in addition to the tones of the organ were the tones of the chimes, forming a beautiful accompaniment. Prayer is like that — it means we are striking the same notes as God. We thus become a part of a universal harmony — the music of the spheres. Our little notes are caught up and universalised. Prayer puts us in tune with the Infinite, and then Infinite power works through our finiteness. Milton summed it up when he said, "By small accomplishing great things."

God invites us not merely to pray, but to make the prayer time a deep encounter with Him. "If my people . . . will . . . pray *and seek my face* . . ." The kind of praying God looks for is not the brief, eager-to-get-it-over-with type, but the unhurried waiting before Him — the true seeking of His face. The Old Testament prophets knew how to pray like this. They came before God and laid hold on Him until something great and mighty happened.

Some time ago, when studying the great Biblical prayers such as the prayer of Moses (Exodus 32:31-32), the prayer of Abraham (Genesis 18:23-33) and the prayer of Daniel (Daniel 9:4-19), I made a fascinating and interesting discovery. I found that in all these prayers there were common elements. The prophets, when they prayed, all used the same principles to get God to respond. Now it follows that if we can discover these common elements, and weave them into our prayers, then their presence will greatly strengthen our petitions.

The first ingredient was selflessness. They put others first — themselves last. The second — boldness. They were so convinced of their cause that they had no fear in coming into His presence. The third ingredient was that of reasoned argument. Taking God's own words, and quoting them back to Him, was one of their greatest strategies. God loves to be reasoned with — "'Come now, let us reason together,' says the Lord . . ." (Isaiah 1:18, NIV). A fourth ingredient of the great Biblical prayers was that of being specific. They knew what they wanted, and they asked God straight out for it. All of these ingredients are in this great prayer of Isaiah:

"Look down from heaven and see
        from your lofty throne, holy and glorious.
Where are your zeal and your might?
Your tenderness and compassion are withheld
        from us.
But you are our Father,
        though Abraham does not know us
        or Israel acknowledge us;
you, O Lord, are our Father,
        our Redeemer from of old is your name.
Why, O Lord, do you make us wander from
        your ways and harden our hearts so we
        do not revere you?

Return for the sake of your servants,
   the tribes that are your inheritance.
For a little while your people
   possessed your holy place,
   but now our enemies have trampled
   down your sanctuary.
We are yours from of old;
   but you have not ruled over them,
   they have not been called by your name."
                        (Isaiah 63:15–19, NIV)

"If my people . . . will humble themselves and
pray . . . *and turn from their wicked ways* . . ." Can
it be true that God's people have wicked ways?
Perhaps the Lord meant careless ways, or formal
ways — surely not wicked ways? The Bible says
wicked ways.

Perhaps we Christians have learned to so
rationalise some of our actions and our behaviour
that we do not realise quite how wicked they
really are. The tendency in this day and age is to
let ourselves off lightly whenever we have done
wrong. We use such euphemisms as: "Well, the
only one I hurt was myself", or: "It isn't all that
important." But any violation of a Biblical
principle is immensely serious. When we pass on
a juicy bit of gossip concerning someone who has
erred and strayed — that is a wicked way. When
we criticise and condemn those who have the
spiritual oversight over us, rather than bring
them before God in prayer — that is a wicked
way. When we wound others by our words or

---

actions, and fail to ask their and God's forgiveness — that is a wicked way. When the acquisition of money dominates our thinking and crowds out eternal things — that is a wicked way. When we watch degrading films or read morally debilitating literature — that is a wicked way.

Can these things, and there are many others, go on in the hearts of those who claim to know the Way — God's own people, called by His Name? I am sorry to say they can. If we are guilty of any of these wicked ways, then let us, here and now, repent of them and have done with them. As the people of God, the world has a right to expect us to be different.

"If my people . . . will humble themselves and pray . . . and turn from their wicked ways, *then will I hear from heaven and will forgive their sin and will heal their land.*"

What a hope-filled promise! What a healing word! "I will hear . . . forgive . . . and heal." Do you believe that? Do you believe that as you prepare your heart through repentance and prayer, God will come again and restore the Church to its former glory? It may be a lot for some of you to believe, especially those of you who find yourselves in a lethargic local church. But not to believe it would make God a liar. Believe it then! With all your heart. Put your whole weight behind the promise. Humble yourself before God. Pray more — in private and in the public prayer meeting. If your church doesn't have a prayer meeting, then gently ask why this is so. Lay hold of the grace of God to get rid of everything in your life of which you know He disapproves. Hear His promise again. Even though you have memorised it, it will do you good to see it spelt out in full:

> "*If my people, who are called by my name, will humble themselves and pray and seek my face and turn from their wicked ways, then will I hear from heaven and will forgive their sin and will heal their land.*"
>
> 2 Chronicles 7:14, NIV

CHAPTER TEN

REVIVAL . . .
A Personal
Checklist

*"Search me, O God, and know
my heart; test me and know my
anxious thoughts."*

(Psalm 139:23, NIV)

Having explored this thrilling and important subject of revival, we need to spend these last few pages giving ourselves a spiritual check-up. It is so easy to allow truth to enter our minds without allowing it to affect our wills. After all, it is only what we act upon that we really believe. It is important to keep in mind, as you go through this check-up, that however deficient you are spiritually, God's love for you remains constant and certain. He loves you as you are, but He loves you too much to let you stay as you are — hence His gentle prodding toward maturity. I say again, it is extremely important that you keep this in mind, otherwise a check-up like this can be devastating, and thus countr-productive.

I must ask myself:

How long is it since I became a Christian? ☐

Have I grown steadily in that time? ☐

Was I ever further forward than I am now? ☐

Can I measure a degree of steady progress in my spiritual understanding? ☐

I wonder how much of my life is left? ☐

Is my reading of the Scriptures a mere duty, or is it a delight? ☐

Am I deeply conscious of the need for more private and corporate prayer? ☐

Do I think more of a larger income than I do of my spiritual development? ☐

Am I a *deeply* spiritual person? ☐

Do I live day by day in conscious dependence on the Lord? ☐

Does the need for revival have much place in my prayer life? ☐

Have I hurt or wounded anyone and not yet apologised? ☐

How much time have I given in the past to acquainting myself with the history of revival? ☐

How much time am I prepared to give in the future? ☐

Do I give myself to God, then draw back when I realise just how much is involved? ☐

How do I feel about undertaking this spiritual check-up — challenged, bored, unconcerned? ☐

Do I grieve when I hear the name of Christ blasphemed, or have I grown insensitive to such things? ☐

When my non-Christian friends ask me about my interests, do I take the opportunity to share Christ? ☐

How long is it since I last shed tears over the condition of the world and the Church? ☐

Am I fighting a losing battle with evil thoughts? ☐

When did I last undertake a spiritual fast? ☐

If I was arrested for being a Christian, would there be enough evidence to convict me? ☐

Am I a faithful steward of the money that flows through my hands? ☐

Do I give at least one-tenth of my income to God? ☐

What do other members of my family think about my Christian life at home? ☐

Does my conscience function in the way God designed it — by objecting to evil and approving good? ☐

Do I watch degrading films in the cinema or on television? ☐

Am I dependent on alcohol to see me through life's problems and difficulties? ☐

Have I debts which are outstanding and well overdue? ☐

Am I honest in relation to my employer — giving my whole energy to my responsibilities, and remembering that I am not employed by an earthly employer, but by God? (Romans 13:1) ☐

Am I eager for revival? ☐

CONCLUSION

REVIVAL . . .
Preparing the
Way

*". . . Prepare the way for the
Lord, make straight paths for
Him."*

(Luke 3:4, NIV)

Nothing else but an extraordinary move of God can meet the urgent need of the Church and the world at this hour.

Evangelism, conferences, seminars, rallies, and the other activities of the Church, while important and necessary, are, however, inadequate in themselves to arrest the attention of an unbelieving world. *God must come down from heaven and visit us in mighty Holy Spirit power.* My personal conviction is that, in conjunction with His prepared people — *He will.*

I was greatly encouraged, when starting on this book, by some words of Bishop Wilberforce. This is what he wrote many years ago: "We look at some mighty estuary which the retiring tide has left bare of water. We see a vast expanse of sand and mud, with little trickling rivulets wearing their scarcely appreciable way through the resisting banks of that yielding ooze. The man who knows not the secrets of the tide, and the influence by which God governs nature would say: How can you expect to see that great expanse covered? But high in the heavens, the unseen Ruler has set the orb, which shall bring in her time, the tides of the surrounding ocean, and when the appointed moment comes, suddenly and sufficiently, the whole is covered by the rejoicing water, and again it is one silvery surface, sandless and mudless — *because the Lord has willed it.*"

My Christian friend, take heart. The unseen Ruler has willed the revival of His people. The day of His power is not far distant. But He looks to you and me to "prepare the way".

PRAYER

Gracious Father, You have given me a commission — a commission to "prepare the way" for the coming revival. I am the wire along which Your power runs. Keep me connected and insulated. For Your praise and honour and glory. Amen.

A SELECTIVE
BIBLIOGRAPHY
ON REVIVAL

Brian Edwards, *Revival! A people saturated with God* (Evangelical Press).

Eifion Evans, *Revival comes to Wales — the story of the 1859 revival in Wales* (Evangelical Press of Wales).

Eifion Evans, *The Welsh Revival of 1904* (Evangelical Press of Wales).

Charles G. Finney, *Finney on Revival* (Bethany House Publishers, USA; Nova Publishing, UK Distributor).

Martyn Lloyd-Jones, *Revival* (Marshall Pickering).

John Pollock, *George Whitefield and the Great Awakening* (Lion Publishing).

Leonard Ravenhill, *Revival Praying* (Bethany House Publishers, USA; Nova Publishing, UK Distributor).

Leonard Ravenhill, *Why Revival Tarries* (Bethany House Publishers, USA; Nova Publishing, UK Distributor).

Emyr Roberts and R. Geraint Gruffydd, *Revival and its Fruit* — two lectures (Evangelical Library of Wales).

Richard Owen Roberts, *Revival* (Tyndale, USA; Scripture Press, UK Distributor).

Mel Tari, *Like A Mighty Wind* (Kingsway Publications Ltd.).

Arthur Wallis, *In the Day of Thy Power* (Christian Literature Crusade).

Colin Whittaker, *Great Revivals* (Marshalls).

Andrew Woolsey, *The Channel of Revival*, a biography of Duncan Campbell (The Faith Mission).

UNDERSTANDING GUIDANCE
Selwyn Hughes

Finding God's will is not about following formulae. It is maintaining a loving relationship with the One who wants to guide us. Upon this foundation Selwyn Hughes takes a careful look at the ways God guides and the freedom He gives for us to choose. A final section offers a practical, step by step guide to knowing God's will.

For publication August 1990

IN HIS IMAGE IN HIS WORLD
A Biblical guide to today's issues
Editor: **Eddie Tait**

In three sections: The World, The Family, The Faith, *In His Image In His World* tackles many of the issues which challenge Christians today. Well-known writers take a fresh look at Scripture on topics like creation/evolution, the environment, politics and power, ethnic peoples, missions, marriage and divorce, sexual relationships, Christianity in the workplace and growing in faith. Eighteen subjects in eighteen chapters, each one divided into seven-day sections with Scripture readings and informed comment — an ideal guide for Bible Study groups or individuals to confront the issues of the 90s.
● Daily readings from the Bible
● Discussion starters for group use

"Bite-sized chunks of thoughtful Biblical material on vital issues. I would recommend it highly for individuals and small groups."
Stephen Gaukroger

"If you are looking for daily Bible-reading notes which cover politics, old age, the green issue and prosperity doctrine, along with 14 other topics, look no further ... this book I liked!"
21st Century Christian